THIS BOOK IS FOR

BORN

LOTS OF LOVE
FORVER & ALWAYS

Made in the USA
Columbia, SC
15 December 2019

84987007R00085